THE DETROIT LIONS

BY THOMAS K. ADAMSON

EPIC

BELLWETHER MEDIA ★ MINNEAPOLIS, MN

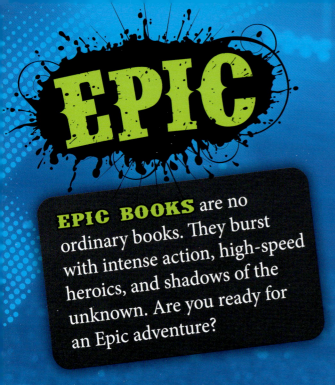

EPIC BOOKS are no ordinary books. They burst with intense action, high-speed heroics, and shadows of the unknown. Are you ready for an Epic adventure?

This book is intended for educational use. Organization and franchise logos are trademarks of the National Football League (NFL). This is not an official book of the NFL. It is not approved by or connected with the NFL.

This edition first published in 2024 by Bellwether Media, Inc.

No part of this publication may be reproduced in whole or in part without written permission of the publisher. For information regarding permission, write to Bellwether Media, Inc., Attention: Permissions Department, 6012 Blue Circle Drive, Minnetonka, MN 55343.

Library of Congress Cataloging-in-Publication Data

Names: Adamson, Thomas K., 1970- author.
Title: The Detroit Lions / by Thomas K. Adamson.
Description: Minneapolis, MN : Bellwether Media, 2024. | Series: Epic. NFL team profiles | Includes bibliographical references and index. | Audience: Ages 7-12 | Audience: Grades 2-3 | Summary: "Engaging images accompany information about the Detroit Lions. The combination of high-interest subject matter and light text is intended for students in grades 2 through 7"-- Provided by publisher.
Identifiers: LCCN 2023021986 (print) | LCCN 2023021987 (ebook) | ISBN 9798886874761 (library binding) | ISBN 9798886876642 (ebook)
Subjects: LCSH: Detroit Lions (Football team)--History--Juvenile literature.
Classification: LCC GV956.D4 A33 2024 (print) | LCC GV956.D4 (ebook) | DDC 796.332/6409774/34--dc23/eng/20230511
LC record available at https://lccn.loc.gov/2023021986
LC ebook record available at https://lccn.loc.gov/2023021987

Text copyright © 2024 by Bellwether Media, Inc. EPIC and associated logos are trademarks and/or registered trademarks of Bellwether Media, Inc.

Editor: Elizabeth Neuenfeldt   Designer: Gabriel Hilger

Printed in the United States of America, North Mankato, MN.

TABLE OF CONTENTS

A BIG TOUCHDOWN	4
THE HISTORY OF THE LIONS	6
THE LIONS TODAY	14
GAME DAY!	16
DETROIT LIONS FACTS	20
GLOSSARY	22
TO LEARN MORE	23
INDEX	24

A BIG TOUCHDOWN

It is the end of the 2022 season. The Lions are playing the Packers. The Packers are winning 16–13. Six minutes remain.

Running back Jamaal Williams gets the ball at the 1-yard line. He runs. **Touchdown**! The Lions go on to win!

JAMAAL WILLIAMS

SPOILER
With this win, the Lions stopped the Packers from making the 2022 season playoffs!

THE HISTORY OF THE LIONS

The Lions were once the Portsmouth Spartans. This National Football League (NFL) team formed in Portsmouth, Michigan, in 1930.

In 1934, a new owner moved the team to Detroit, Michigan. The Lions won the NFL **championship** the next year.

1935 LIONS GAME

LIONS AND TIGERS

The new owner changed the team's name to the Lions. This went well with the baseball team in Detroit, the Tigers.

DETROIT, MICHIGAN

The Lions were one of the best teams in the 1950s. They beat the Cleveland Browns for the NFL championship three times. Their last championship win was in 1957.

1953 NFL CHAMPIONSHIP GAME

1962 LIONS GAME

From 1958 to 1981, the team struggled. They only reached the **playoffs** once.

In 1989, running back Barry Sanders joined the team. He helped the team reach the NFC Championship Game in the 1991 season. But they lost.

BARRY SANDERS IN THE 1991 NFC CHAMPIONSHIP GAME

The Lions made the playoffs five more times in the 1990s. But they lost every playoff game.

1994 PLAYOFF GAME

In 2009, **quarterback** Matthew Stafford joined the Lions. He and **wide receiver** Calvin Johnson led the Lions through promising seasons.

MATTHEW STAFFORD

CALVIN JOHNSON

12

They still could not get a playoff win. The team is still working toward its first **Super Bowl**.

WINLESS SEASON

In 2008, the Lions hit an all-time low. They finished the season with the NFL's first 0–16 record.

TROPHY CASE

NFL championships
4

NFL NATIONAL DIVISION championships
1

NFC CENTRAL championships
3

PLAYOFF appearances
17

13

THE LIONS TODAY

LIONS VS. PACKERS

The Lions play their home games at Ford Field in Detroit, Michigan. They are part of the NFC North **division**.

The other NFC North teams are all **rivals**. But the biggest is the Green Bay Packers.

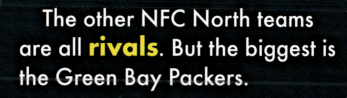

FORD FIELD

Detroit, Michigan

GAME DAY!

The Lions play a home game every Thanksgiving Day.

This **tradition** started in 1934. The new owner was trying to draw more fans. The game was heard on radios all over the country!

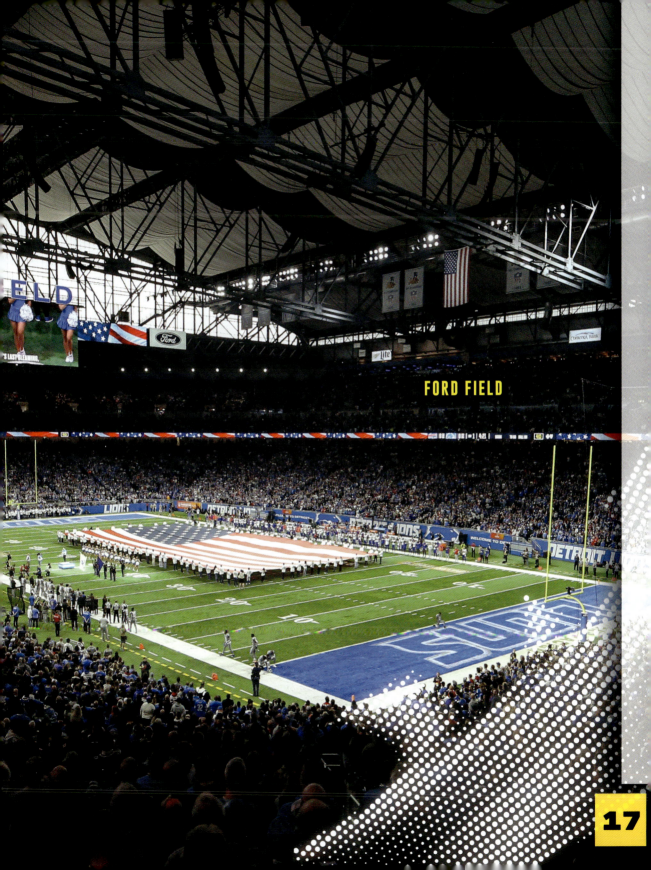

The Lions fight song plays when the Lions score. Theo "Gridiron" Spight leads the singing. He then shouts, "Go Lions!"

Lions fans are proud of the team's past success. They support their team every year!

THEO "GRIDIRON" SPIGHT

FAMOUS PLAYERS

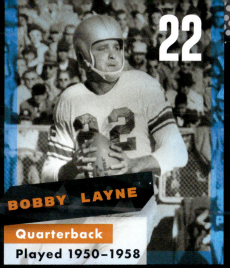

22

BOBBY LAYNE
Quarterback
Played 1950–1958

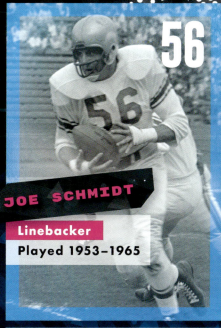

56

JOE SCHMIDT
Linebacker
Played 1953–1965

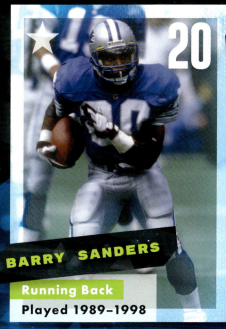

20

BARRY SANDERS
Running Back
Played 1989–1998

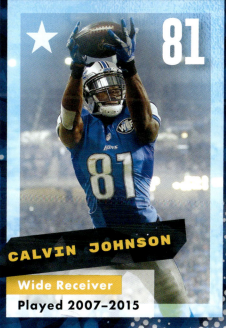

81

CALVIN JOHNSON
Wide Receiver
Played 2007–2015

9

MATTHEW STAFFORD
Quarterback
Played 2009–2020

DETROIT LIONS FACTS

LOGO

JOINED THE NFL	1930

NICKNAME	Silver Crush

MASCOT — ROARY

CONFERENCE
National Football Conference (NFC)

COLORS

DIVISION | NFC North

 Chicago Bears
 Green Bay Packers
 Minnesota Vikings

STADIUM

★ FORD FIELD ★
opened August 24, 2002

holds **65,000** people

20

🕐 TIMELINE

1934 — The team is renamed the Detroit Lions

1957 — The Lions win their fourth NFL Championship Game

1989 — Barry Sanders joins the Lions

1992 — The Lions play in the NFC Championship Game

2009 — Matthew Stafford joins the Lions

★ RECORDS ★

All-Time Passing Leader

Matthew Stafford
45,109 yards

All-Time Rushing Leader
Barry Sanders
15,269 yards

All-Time Receiving Leader
Calvin Johnson
11,619 yards

All-Time Scoring Leader
Jason Hanson
2,150 points

21

GLOSSARY

championship—a contest to decide the best team or person

division—a group of NFL teams from the same area that often play against each other; there are eight divisions in the NFL.

playoffs—games played after the regular NFL season is over; playoff games determine which teams play in the championship game.

quarterback—a player whose main job is to throw and hand off the ball

rivals—long-standing opponents

running back—a player whose main job is to run with the ball

Super Bowl—the annual championship game of the NFL

touchdown—a score that occurs when a team crosses into their opponent's end zone with the football; a touchdown is worth six points.

tradition—a special way people celebrate or honor something

wide receiver—a player whose main job is to catch passes from the quarterback

TO LEARN MORE

AT THE LIBRARY

Abdo, Kenny. *Detroit Lions*. Minneapolis, Minn.: Abdo Zoom, 2022.

Lowe, Alexander. *G.O.A.T. Football Running Backs*. Minneapolis, Minn.: Lerner Publications, 2023.

Scheff, Matt. *Matthew Stafford*. Lake Elmo, Minn.: Focus Readers, 2023.

ON THE WEB

FACTSURFER

Factsurfer.com gives you a safe, fun way to find more information.

1. Go to www.factsurfer.com.

2. Enter "Detroit Lions" into the search box and click 🔍.

3. Select your book cover to see a list of related content.

INDEX

colors, 20

Detroit, Michigan, 6, 7, 14, 15

Detroit Lions facts, 20–21

famous players, 19

fans, 16, 18

fight song, 18

Ford Field, 14, 15, 17, 20

history, 4, 5, 6, 7, 8, 9, 10, 11, 12, 13, 16

Johnson, Calvin, 12

mascot, 20

name, 7

National Football League (NFL), 6, 13, 20

NFC Championship Game, 10

NFC North, 14, 15, 20

NFL championship, 6, 8

playoffs, 5, 9, 11, 13

Portsmouth Spartans, 6

positions, 5, 10, 12

records, 13, 21

rival, 15

Sanders, Barry, 10

Spight, Theo "Gridiron," 18

Stafford, Matthew, 12

Super Bowl, 13

Thanksgiving Day, 16

timeline, 21

trophy case, 13

Williams, Jamaal, 5

The images in this book are reproduced through the courtesy of: Cooper Neill/ AP Images, cover (hero); Bryan Pollard, cover (stadium); Rey Del Rio/ Contributor/ Getty, p. 3; Matt Ludtke/ AP Images, p. 4; Morry Gash/ AP Images, p. 5; ASSOCIATED PRESS/ AP Images, p. 6; f11photo, pp. 6-7; George Gelatly/ Contributor/ Getty, p. 8; Focus On Sport/ Contributor/ Getty, pp. 9, 19 (Barry Sanders), 21 (Barry Sanders); Doug Mills/ AP Images, p. 10; Betsy Peabody Rowe/ Contributor/ Getty, pp. 10-11; NurPhoto/ Contributor/ Getty, p. 12; Gregory Shamus/ Stringer/ Getty, pp. 12 (inset), 19 (Calvin Johnson, Matthew Stafford), 21 (Calvin Johnson); Mike Mulholland/ Stringer/ Getty, p. 14; NurPhoto SRL/ Alamy, p. 15 (Ford Field); NFL/ Wikipedia, pp. 15 (Lions logo), 19 (Lions logo, Bears logo, Packers logo, Vikings logo, NFC logo); Icon Sportswire/ Contributor/ Getty, pp. 16, 16-17, 20 (mascot); Carlos Osorio/ AP Images, pp. 18-19; Bettmann/ Contributor/ Getty, p. 19 (Bobby Layne); The Enthusiast Network/ Contributor/ Getty, p. 19 (Joe Schmidt); Grindstone Media Group, p. 20 (stadium); Sports Studio Photos/ Contributor/ Getty, p. 21 (1934); Scott Boehm/ AP Images, p. 21 (1957); JOHN STORMZAND/ AP Images, p. 21 (1989); Greg Gibson/ AP Images, p. 21 (1992); Jeff Zelevansky/ Stringer/ Getty, p. 21 (2009); Leon Halip/ Contributor/ Getty, p. 21 (Matthew Stafford); Harry How/ Staff/ Getty, p. 21 (Jason Hanson).